Give Your Dog a Bone Series

THE SECRET TO GETTING YOUR DOG TO DO WHAT YOU WANT

JennaLee Gallicchio

.　　.　　.　　.　　.

Published by
From Puppy To Pal Productions
Bedminster, NJ
FromPuppyToPal.com

.　　.　　.　　.　　.

Print Layout by
N.D. Author Services [NDAS]
www.NDAuthorServices.com

ALSO BY JENNALEE GALLICCHIO

Teach Your Dog To Pee and Poop Outside: Housetraining Made Easy

How to Turn Your Problem Pup into Your Dream Dog

DEDICATION

The Secret To Getting Your Dog To Do What You Want is dedicated to my dog, Mattie. Without him coming into my life and challenging me to change, I wouldn't have been inspired to be living my passion today. Nor would I have learned the secret that would transform our lives. Thank you Mattie-Matt for coming into my life and turning it upside down. It has been a life changing journey and I am so glad that you chose me to take it with. You are forever in my heart. Ryder and I miss you!

THANKS

As always, I want to thank my wonderful, supportive, crazy family. You have been there through all of it and your support is more important to me than I can ever say. I love you!

I would like to thank Cathleen Campbell, my fantabulous EFT Practitioner! I don't know how I would've made it through these last few years if not for your guidance and help. Our sessions have proved invaluable to me!

Thank you, Angela Treat Lyon, for doing the Kindle Course! It gave me the tools and courage I needed to keep it simple and 'just do it'! Your help has been tremendous and generous beyond belief.

Thank you to all the dogs who I've been fortunate enough to work with and learn from. And, most importantly, to their owners who do me the greatest honor by hiring me. It has been my extreme pleasure and greatest joy.

Contents

Chapter 1:
  WHY GIVE YOUR DOG A BONE............................3
Chapter 2:
  WHY REWARDS ARE IMPORTANT..........................9
Chapter 3:
  DO I NEED TO REWARD EVERYTIME?...................13
Chapter 4:
  HOW ARE WE REWARED? 17
Chapter 5:
  WRITING YOUR DOG'S PAYCHECK.......................19
Chapter 6:
  WAITING FOR THE RAIN................................23
Chapter 7:
  EXAMPLES TO GET YOU STARTED 27
Chapter 8:
  NOW WHAT?..35
GLOSSARY...39
DON'T MISS!..41
URGENT PLEA!..42
ABOUT THE AUTHOR.....................................43

CHAPTER 1:
WHY GIVE YOUR DOG A BONE

WHAT I LEARNED WHEN TRAINING MATTIE

"The journey of a thousand miles begins with one step."
—Lao Tzu

My story starts when I adopted a puppy who was out of control. I knew that if I didn't do something I would have to return him. I felt so ashamed and like a failure. But, in reality, I was overwhelmed and frustrated. When I say I've been in the shoes of my clients, it's because I have.

When I adopted Mattie, I thought I understood and knew dogs. I had trained Sydney, my current dog at the time, and figured I knew what I was doing. In fact, I thought I was a dog expert. Hindsight is 20/20 and, looking back at that now, I can see how naive my thinking was. Boy oh boy, did Mattie have a thing or two to teach me about me being an 'expert'!

Mattie was distant, fearful, unloving and independent. He wanted nothing to do with me and I had no clue how to reach him. It felt like I was living with an autistic child. After 6 months, I almost called it quits. I was frustrated, overwhelmed and in over my head.

When my 6 year old dog Sydney died suddenly, I was devastated. The dog I adored was gone and I was left with a dog I didn't like, forget about love. But I was also left with no excuses. Making things work with Mattie became a priority and I was on a mission.

When I started training Mattie, I was coming from a perspective of 'my dog should do what I want because I want him to'. Anyone else been there? Sydney did that; Ryder (my current puppy) would probably do that; Mattie, on the other hand, wasn't that type of dog.

Mattie did what he wanted to do, because he wanted to do it. If there were negative consequences, he thought about it after the fact or not at all. He was in the moment and very independent—yet very soft, temperament wise, I learned later.

The fact that he had no need for me, other than the meal I could feed him, (which he didn't like all that much) made training very difficult. At that time, I didn't understand or know about controlling resources and gave him whatever his heart desired. That was one of many mistakes I was making.

That was over 11 years ago and, since then, my life and how I train dogs has changed drastically.

In my training adventures, with Mattie and my clients, I've learned there is a lot of confusion about what a reward is and isn't. Most people think that a reward is a treat and only a treat. But a reward is whatever our dog enjoys doing or receiving.

I've learned that some people have a very difficult time rewarding their dogs and usually aren't rewarding frequently enough, while others are rewarding behaviors they don't want. I have also learned that rewards are different for each dog and are more than just treats.

A run in a field; chasing a lure; a game of chase; playing fetch, tug, food or a bone; even a smile or a word of praise—if your dog finds it rewarding, then it is and can be used as a reward.

Our dog needs to like getting it, in exchange for offering a behavior that we want. In order for it to work, the reward needs to have value to our pup.

What I learned in my mission—on how to get through to Mattie—changed my life. Mattie was a tough cookie and one of the greatest gifts that he helped me to achieve was patience. He suffered from anxiety, so whenever we were in a new environment he would shut down and not eat.

I had to learn how to get creative with rewards for him. For example, he always wanted to move forward and he usually liked to do it while 'screaming' and pulling on the leash. To counteract this, I would stop and wait for him to sit and be calm. Later, I required him to give me eye contact before we could keep going forward. As a reward, he got to move forward and continue walking.

The calm, quiet was what I wanted and the moving forward was what he wanted. So I used the moving forward as the reward. As we both got into the habit, it became much easier to reinforce it and Mattie got much better at walking on the leash.

Before Mattie passed away, I was able to fully see the transformation that our lives had taken. Mattie went from a distant, independent dog, to a dog who loved to snuggle next to me. He helped to teach our new four legged pack member, Ryder, so many things, including the importance of being calm while getting the leash on.

I was really lucky to have such an incredible teacher in my life and I am grateful that I was a willing student.

Seeing how Mattie was transformed and how my life was changed, has inspired me to help people like you. In being given this gift of opportunity and learning, I hope to help you and others know the joy that I experience with Ryder, and was lucky enough to experience with Mattie, daily.

Happy Training!

Jenna

CHAPTER 2:
WHY REWARDS ARE IMPORTANT

"Rewards let your dog know when they make the right choices. The more the right choice is rewarded, the more frequently it will occur."
—JennaLee Gallicchio

Rewards are an integral part of learning. We all become better learners when we are praised and rewarded for a behavior that we are doing.

For example, when was the last time you learned something new? Did you have someone encouraging you or telling you what was wrong?

I know that, when I am learning something, I am much more willing if I am being encouraged. In fact, it usually gets me excited about learning the new skill. If the teacher can make what I am learning feel like a game, so much the better!

How our dogs learn isn't much different. When we are encouraging and rewarding our dogs for the behaviors we want, they tend to want to do those behaviors more often. If you can learn to make training fun and feel like a game, your dog will want to work with you whenever they have the chance.

Why? Because "playing" is fun and we all like to play. When training feels like work, or a J-O-B, we all get bored and uninspired. By learning how to make work equal play and play equal work, you will find yourself with a dog who can't seem to get enough of you.

The key to turning training into a game is figuring out what rewards your dog wants and enjoys. Pay attention to how your pup responds to a ball, a treat, or your praise, just to name a few. Use the things that make your dog go wild! This will keep your pup engaged with you when training.

Why? Because it will feel like a game and games are fast and exciting. Which is why we all love a good game.

Do you remember that one teacher that you absolutely adored? The one whose class you couldn't wait to arrive at and get to "work"? If you were lucky, you had more than one of those. Let yourself go back in time and remember that feeling. How do you feel?

I remember my kindergarten and third grade teacher, Mrs. Grazia. I LOVED going to her class! I still remember wanting to run to her class and couldn't wait to be around her. I had a cheerleading coach named Lynn who was like that too.

They didn't make what I did easy, but they did make what we did fun! They are also people I will never forget. They are people who inspired me.

That's the relationship I want for you and your dog. I want a relationship where you can't wait to "work" with them and when you do, you are so in the moment that time just seems to fly.

I know that you can have exactly that! How do I know? Because I do. Training, for me, is such a complete joy! I love being able to "work" with Ryder. I love when the light bulb goes off and what we're doing clicks. But, even more, I love that I can laugh at both of our mistakes and appreciate our efforts.

Training, for me, is fun and that is what I want for you. Reach for it, strive for it, let it change your life! You will wonder how you ever lived without it before.

Now for the question I get asked a lot!

CHAPTER 3:
DO I NEED TO
REWARD EVERYTIME?

TO REWARD OR NOT REWARD? THAT IS *NEVER* THE QUESTION.

"Typically, if you reward something, you get more of it. You punish something, you get less of it..."
—Daniel H. Pink

Before I answer that question, I want to re-clarify what a reward is and what a reward isn't.

A reward is anything that an animal or a human (yes I meant to say human) finds reinforcing and encourages a behavior to keep occurring. What that reward is, will vary from one individual to another. The same thing applies to dogs. Some dogs love fetch, while others may love going for a swim or like lying in the sun.

13

When you say "reward", most people think food, but food isn't the only reward. Food is the easiest, because most dogs like it and will work for it. But it is not the ONLY reward we can use. In fact, it is just one of many rewards at our disposal.

A reward can be a treat, praise, going outside for a walk, a toy, your attention (praise or yelling, your pup doesn't see them as different), giving in to whining, begging or ANYTHING your dog likes or wants.

The key word to remember here is **DOG**. Your **DOG**, **not YOU**, has to believe the reward is worth the effort it takes to give you the behavior you want. It isn't something you THINK your dog SHOULD like, but something your dog DOES like.

Remember, your attention—in whatever form, from yelling to praising—is rewarding to your dog. It is a good idea to use my mantra of "reward what you want and ignore what you don't" wisely.

If you aren't using it already, I suggest that you put it into practice today. Just this small change will have a massive effect on your dog's behavior.

So, back to the question: "Do I need to reward every time?" If you haven't guessed it yet, my answer is yes, you do. At this point, you should also realize that, when I say "reward", I am talking about a whole box full of tools that you can use.

Pick and choose how and when you use the re-wards. By using them consistently, you will encour-age your pup to keep offering behaviors you want to keep happening.

CHAPTER 4:
HOW ARE WE
REWARED?

SHOW ME THE MONEY!

"Shopping at any level is a bit of therapy for my medulla oblongata."
—Theophilus London

We go to work 5 days a week for a paycheck. Work is not the reward; work is what we have to do to get the paycheck. The paycheck is not really the reward, either. It's the THINGS we get to BUY or DO with the paycheck that is OUR reward.

That new pair of shoes, a day at the beach, a house, a new car, the food in the refrigerator, or possibly even putting it into a savings account—it is different from person to person and it is different from dog to dog.

Another way to think of it is getting free concert tickets. Not just FREE tickets, but box seats AND you get to meet the artist. Sounds great, right?! But what if it's someone you really don't want to see or —even worse—a band you HATE?

How much are those tickets worth to you now? Not much. Plus, you went from being super excited to totally bummed! In fact, you are completely disappointed. That is why dogs stop sitting or laying down when you ask them.

CHAPTER 5: WRITING YOUR DOG'S PAYCHECK

APPLYING THIS SAME THEORY TO YOUR DOG.

"Isn't it funny how a bear loves honey?
Buzz. Buzz. Buzz. I wonder why he
does?"
—Winnie The Pooh

You have a couch potato who likes nothing more than a good treat and you try to reward her with fetch. "What?" she says, "They know I HATE fetch... Where's my cookie? Last time I get off the couch for that!" The next time you ask for the "sit" or the "down", they stare at you blankly, like they've never heard the word before.

Bringing it back to work. If you HATE your job, it doesn't matter how much they pay you, you won't enjoy getting up in the morning to go to the office.

The paycheck will probably keep you coming back, but it won't make you enjoy the task at hand.

If your dog's paycheck isn't good enough, it doesn't matter what you do, they won't even show up at the office for work.

I can't say this enough; a reward is whatever your dog thinks is a paycheck worth working for. Calm behavior while getting their leash on so they can go for a walk, YES! Walk =YAY! Sitting when asked on the walk, so that they can start moving again. Treats, balls—if your dog LIKES them, they will work.

Eventually, a reward can even be a smile and a "Good Job"... IF your dog likes it.

Think about what YOU consider rewarding for your dog; now pay attention to what your DOG finds rewarding. Once you figure this out, keep the paycheck and the bonuses coming consistently.

By doing this, you will notice that your dog not only shows up to the office, but is actually EXCITED about the work you ask them to do!

Try to look at a reward as an exchange for services. Each recipient needs to find value in what they are receiving.

CHAPTER 6: WAITING FOR THE RAIN

LET THE REWARDS RAIN DOWN

"If a dogs prayers were answered bones would rain from the sky."
—Proverb

People are always asking me when they can stop rewarding a behavior, to which I reply, "How much do you want the behavior to continue?" For some reason, many people have a difficult time at the thought of rewarding 'forever'. I'm not sure why, but they do.

The bottom line is this: behavior that is rewarded on a consistent basis is behavior that will be repeated. If you want a behavior to continue, then you will want to keep rewarding it.

The best way to make this happen is to teach your dog to "Wait for the rain". I know it sounds weird, but we always know that it will rain sooner or later, right? It has to. It is the way of the world, a constant, a known fact.

We want to teach our dog that the rewards WILL rain down on them. When they expect that a reward is coming, they will almost always choose to offer the behavior.

I say almost because nobody, not even us, does anything 100% percent all of the time. We may try, but that would require perfection and one thing we are not is perfect. Neither is our dog.

Being consistent in the beginning—and for some time after that—is extremely important. Trust takes time to build. We need to see that someone is consistent in their actions. You need to build this trust in your dog.

Once they believe it WILL rain, that's when the magic happens. How long it takes is based on how consistent you are and your dog's ability to trust. How long it takes is how long it takes and each dog is different.

For example, you believe that you are getting paid for going to work, it's why you show up. But what if you went to work and your boss told you he was going to pay you next week? You would probably be annoyed, but you would believe him

.

Now, what if he told you the week after that he would pay you next week? You would start to have doubts, right? If he told you the week after that that he would pay you NEXT week, you'd be off looking for another job.

Why? Because you no longer believe or trust him to be able to pay you. The same is true for your dog.

Your dog needs to trust and believe that it WILL rain or that they will get paid. There must not be any doubt in their mind and, if there is, they will be looking for another job or, more precisely, a behavior that does pay them.

How do I make my dog believe? Be consistent and continue to reward until your dog offers a behavior 8 out of 10 times, or 80%. When this happens, you can start to reward every other time, or every third time, but until they are at 80% it is in your best interest to reward every time.

Remember, you are letting your dog know that there is no doubt that that paycheck is coming.

CHAPTER 7:
EXAMPLES TO GET YOU STARTED

"Once our dog understands that their behavior is the key to what happens next that's when the fun begins."
—JennaLee Gallicchio

CALM AND QUIET GETS THE WALK

Does your dog get excited when you get ready for a walk? Jump? Bark? Circle? The reason is that our dogs find going for a walk ridiculously exciting. So exciting in fact, that it is actually a reward. If you are not using this reward to your advantage, you are missing out.

One of the requirements in my household is that only four paws on the floor will get the leash and harness on. I like calm and quiet behaviors and I work really hard to reinforce them, or reward them, as often as possible.

This is one of the easiest things to change if your dog is acting crazy. You just need to be consistent.

Follow the steps below, have patience and watch the transformation. You will be amazed and con-vinced.

Before beginning you will want to:

First, make sure your dog has gone to the bathroom. We don't want to do this when they haven't gone—that's just asking for accidents.

Second, make sure you have ample time to do this. A weekend or evening when you have an hour or more is best. If you stay calm and don't get frustrat-ed, this will work better for you.

This is really so simple you're going to wonder why you didn't think of it yourself.

1. Get the leash.

2. If your dog does anything other than stand quietly, put the leash back without saying a word.

3. Repeat Steps 1 & 2 until your dog is standing quietly.

When your dog is standing quietly, it's time to move on to the next steps.

4. Try to hook the leash to your dog's collar.

5. Repeat Step 2.

6. Repeat Step 3.

That's it! Simple isn't it?! You can go to my YouTube channel, AllStarPaws, and watch Door Manners Step 1 to see what the end result looks like as Mattie (off Screen), Ryder and I get ready for a walk.

Leashes are just no longer exciting in my house.

POLITE DINING - CALM AND QUIET GETS THE MEAL.

When it's time for Ryder to eat at my house I ask that he is sitting or standing quietly while I am getting his meal ready. For Ryder this was hard initially because he LOVES his food so much! He would jump all over and run to the cabinet where his food was, even sometimes bark in his excitement.

It was actually very cute especially when he was so small but I knew that it wasn't a behavior that I wanted when he was full grown.

Because he would get easily excited I had to make sure that I was being very clear. What clear means is that anytime Ryder got to close to the food bag or to close to me while I was mixing his food, I would stop and back away from the counter.

Sometimes I would even walk out the room and then come back. If he was standing or sitting quietly I would continue mixing up his food.

If your dog is acting crazy while you are getting his meal ready and you keep doing it, what are you telling him? That his behavior is acceptable of course. So lets talk about how to change that, so that your pup is waiting quietly for his meal to be served.

Do this at every meal and it will be no time at all before you are seeing a change. Remember that it is important that you are really clear at stopping when any behavior you don't want is happening and starting up again when behavior you want is.

This exercise is done like the leash, your actions speak louder than your words. Which means you don't want to tell your dog what to do.

1. Start getting their meal together. Grab their bowl, go to the fridge or the food bag, whatever your normal routine is.

2. If your dog does anything other than stand or sit quietly, stop the routine and leave. Walk out of the room. When your dog follows you as if to say "Huh?" go back to the kitchen.

3. Repeat Steps 1 & 2 until your dog is standing or sitting quietly. (Sound familiar?)

Keep up with steps 1 and 2 until you are actually finished getting their meal ready. When you are finished move on to step 4.

4. Stand holding your dogs bowl up and wait for them to sit (let your dog think it out – don't tell them. This may take a while at first so be

patient).

5. Slowly start to lower the bowl. When your dog gets up, stand back up and repeat Step 4. This point is their tolerance point.

6. Repeat Steps 4 & 5 . Start to pay attention to exactly how far you can lower the bowl before your dog gets up. Once you know the point where your dog will get up from the sit stop BE-FORE you get there.

7. When your pup is sitting with the bowl low-ered at their tolerance point, say "Get It'" and lower the bowl to the floor.

It is important to **stop moving** and **to say** "Get It" **before** lowering the bowl to the floor. If you don't follow these steps then your dog won't understand that their sitting quietly and **waiting** is what gets them their food.

Instead they will think that diving for it is the ac-ceptable behavior because that's what you are unin-tentionally rewarding.

Keep working slowly to get the bowl closer and clos-er to being on the floor. Once you can get it to the floor start making them wait a bit longer before let-ting them get it. You can also add them looking at you first as the cue to say 'get it'.

Just remember to move at your dogs pace and don't rush. I won't say that meal times aren't completely unexciting in my house, since Ryder is still learning, but they are calm and quiet.

THINGS YOUR DOG MIGHT FIND REWARDING.

Here are just a few ideas to help you get started when working to figure out what your dog really likes.

1. A walk.

2. A good run.

3. A game of tug.

4. Chase.

5. Going for a swim.

6. Treats.

7. A bone.

8. Hide and Seek

9. Praise (both verbal and physical petting)

10.   Fetch

11.   Sniffing

12.   Greeting a person.

13.   Squeaky toy

14.   Stuffed toy

15.   Playing with you.

Try these out and pay attention to how your dog re-sponds. If they come back for more - jackpot! You've got a winner. If not, try another one. Keep trying until you find the ones that get them excited and coming back for more. It will help if you get excited too. The more fun you are, the more fun your dog will have.

If you can get 10 or more rewards on your list, it will only help you. It may take a little time and investi-gating but it will be well worth the effort. Once you have your list safe guard these rewards and don't let your dog have free access to them.

Something that we get to have all the time loses its value once we get bored with it. The same is true for our dogs. Guard your dog's choice of reward like a pot of gold and use them wisely.

CHAPTER 8: NOW WHAT?

"The End is Only The beginning."
-Evy, The Mummy

Now you get to take what you've learned and apply it to your dog. Let's review.

I talked about what a reward is and isn't. I asked you to look at how you like to be rewarded and what you consider a reward.

I then asked you to apply that same concept to your dog and their "rewards".

Lastly, I covered how you can let your dog know that there will always be a payday for them.

Once we truly understand the value that our pup puts on their toys, food, a ball, etc., then we have the key to getting our dog to do what we want every time—use it to your advantage.

The more we use what our dog values as a reward, the more value our dog will put on us because of our association with their favorite things!

Remember me mentioning your favorite teacher and how much fun you had in their class? Be that teacher for your dog!

You just need to put in a little time and effort to find out what value your pup puts on the rewards you give them. Once you know what your dog values, you will have more power to affect the behaviors your dog offers.

Understanding why you are getting more of the same, good or bad, will give you the ability to influence that. Being alert and aware to this simple concept will help you notice subtle shifts in your dogs behavior and will help you to be better at predicting how your dog will respond.

Training is supposed to be fun and a way to truly connect with your dog. When you and your dog can't wait to get to class, then you will know you are doing it right! The whole point of having a dog is to love and enjoy them.

Now you know the secret to be able to do just that, you can help to influence the behaviors you want and are most important to you.

What are you waiting for? Start to learn about your dog now. Get a list together of what your dog loves and begin using it to your advantage. Most importantly, have fun!

I'd love to hear from you about how this book has helped you and any experiences you've had with applying this to your training routine!

Send me an email at: Jenna@AllStarPaws.com or visit me on Facebook page at All Star Paws Dog Training or JennaLee Gallicchio and tell me all about it.

If you are interested in additional training please visit AllStarPawsAcademy.com to check out my online programs and FREE videos or visit AllStarPaws.com if you would like to work with me privately.

GLOSSARY

REWARD

I added the glossary for you to make sure you truly understand the concept of rewarding your dog. Sometimes learning the definition helps people to understand a word better and that can help to understand the application. I chose a few definitions thinking that hearing them said in different ways might help. I know that helps me.

re·ward (noun)
(rĭ-wôrd′)

1. A consequence that happens to someone as a result of worthy or unworthy behavior: the rewards of exercise; the rewards of lying to your boss.

2. Money offered or given for some special service, such as the return of a lost article or the capture of a criminal.

3. A satisfying return on investment; a profit.

4. Psychology The return for performance of a desired behavior; positive reinforcement.
tr.v. re·ward·ed, re·ward·ing, re·wards
To give a reward to or for.

*****

reward (verb)
re·ward \ri-'wòrd\

Simple Definition of reward

: to give money or another kind of payment to (someone or something) for something good that has been done

Source: Merriam-Webster's Learner's Dictionary

*****

reward (noun)
re·ward \ri-wawrd\

-something given or received in return or recompense for service, merit, hardship, etc.
verb (used with object)

-to recompense or requite (a person or animal) for service, merit, achievement, etc.

-to make return for or requite (service, merit, etc.); recompense.

Source: American Psychological Association (APA):

reward. (n.d.). Collins English Dictionary - Complete & Unabridged 10th Edition. Retrieved April 27, 2016 from Dictionary.com website http://www.dictionary.-com/browse/reward

*****

reward (noun)
/rɪ'wɔrd/

- something given in exchange for a useful idea, good behavior, excellent work, etc.

Source: Definition of reward from the Cambridge Academic Content Dictionary © Cambridge University Press

DON'T MISS!

If you just got a new puppy or a new dog and need help with housetraining, get **Teach Your Dog To Pee and Poop Outside: Housetraining Made Easy**. It is available in print, on Amazon Kindle and Audible.com. There is also an online program on AllStarPawsAcademy.com.

These books are in the works and you won't want to miss them:

Turn Your Problem Pup Into Your Dream Dog

HELP! My Dog Won't Stop (Insert Behavior Here)!

Register at JennaLeeGallicchio.com to be notified of all new releases. Your dog will thank you!

URGENT PLEA!

Will You Help?

Thank you for reading Jenna's (my mom's) book! It will really help her to buy me lots of bones.

Would you kindly go back to the site where you purchased this book and leave your feedback? It helps my mom (Jenna) to make sure that she is presenting you the information in a way that is helpful to you. It will also let her know what you want so she can help you better.

If you bought this book in a store stop by her Facebook page: Facebook.com/AllStarPaws and let her know what you thought.

ABOUT THE AUTHOR

In 2004, JennaLee Gallicchio was working in the Banking Industry as a Sales Assistant. Although not happy, she had no thought of changing careers. All that changed when she adopted a four month old puppy who would turn her world upside down. His name was Mattie.

Mattie left Jenna feeling overwhelmed, frustrated and in way over her head. It wasn't just Jenna he left feeling this way, but also her family, who all had their own dogs.

Close to deciding that the best thing would be to return him to the dog rescue where she adopted him, she decided to try one thing first. In a desperate effort, she hired a professional dog trainer, K9 Experience.

While just starting to work with Kay Anne, her dog, Sydney, died very suddenly. Extremely saddened by her loss, she also acknowledged to herself that she had no excuses and failing to make a change with Mattie was not an option.

Working with K9 Experience gave Jenna and Mattie a great start and also renewed Jenna's own personal passion for training dogs.

Completing a certification program, through Animal Behavior College, she began teaching group classes at The Barker Lounge in Roselle, NJ. She also continued to take classes with Mattie where they continued to build their relationship.

She completed Camp R.E.W.A.R.D. with Pamela Dennison and worked for a short time with Tracy Sklenar and MaryLou Hanlin, in the hopes of doing Agility. As she saw the transformation in Mattie, Jenna was inspired, even more, to learn more about the "science" behind the training. It is a road she has never looked back on.

Although Mattie is no longer with her, he left a lasting impact on her life. Because of his needs, Jenna now has the ability to teach clients how to really understand and learn from their dogs. Sharing with them and inspiring them is an extreme pleasure.

She was fortunate enough to use this training when Ryder joined her and then again with Emmy. Having a puppy is a humbling experience and it was one that was filled with laughter, and tears of frustration at times.

This is Jenna's first instructional training book. but she has many others in her head and in the works.

Thank you again to all of the wonderful readers who have taken the time to read this! It means more than you will ever know.

This book is also available in a Kindle edition or Audio form. Both can be found on Amazon.com.

ADDITIONAL BOOKS AVAILABLE:

TEACH YOUR DOG TO PEE AND POOP OUTSIDE: HOUSETRAINING MADE EASY